How

To Make Money

Online

By

Peter Duncan

TABLE OF CONTENTS

Introduction

Making money online has gained popularity in today's digital world. *There are various ways to make money online, including freelance work, e-commerce, affiliate marketing,* and online advertising. Nevertheless, with so many choices, it can be difficult to know where to begin. This book will examine numerous internet income streams and offer you insights, pointers, and useful guides to help you reach your financial objectives.

Chapter 1

Online Money Making

The Advantages of Earning Money Online

Making money online has several advantages, such as:

Flexibility: One of the main benefits of earning money online is the amount of freedom it provides. Since you can work from anywhere and at any time, you can juggle work with other commitments and your personal life.

Potential for higher income: Compared to typical occupations, earning money online has a higher earning potential. A larger earning potential can result from the ability to frequently work for several clients or generate multiple sources of income.

Minimal startup costs: Setting up an online business or operating as a freelancer sometimes just requires a little amount of capital. It is accessible to a larger group of individuals because all you need is a computer and an internet connection.

Many opportunities: From starting a blog to selling goods on an e-commerce site, there are countless methods to earn money online. This means you can locate a job that fits your interests and skill set.

more autonomy: When you earn a living online, you frequently decide what you do and when. This may result in a rise in autonomy and a feeling of fulfillment.

Better work-life balance: Working online can frequently help you have a better work-life balance. Work can be scheduled around responsibilities to your family and other obligations, which can reduce stress and improve general well-being.

Nevertheless, there are many advantages to earning money online, including increased income, freedom, and a better quality of life.

*The Difficulties of Internet Money Making

Although it might seem like a good concept, making money online has its own set of challenges. The following are some of the biggest challenges you could run against when trying to earn money online: Internet businesses must contend with fierce competition, which can make it difficult to stand out and attract customers or clients.

Trust issues: People sometimes find it difficult to trust online businesses or persons since the internet is so big. It may take some time and work to win over your audience's trust.

Technical expertise: Depending on the kind of online business you plan to launch, you may require technical expertise in areas like web development, graphic design, or search engine optimization. You may need to spend time and money learning these talents if you don't already have them, or you may need to hire someone who does.

Algorithm updates can have a significant effect on your traffic and profitability if you rely on social media or search engine traffic to bring users to your website.

Distractions: Working online, especially if you do it from home, can be annoying. To stay focused, you might need to practice self-control and establish a regular schedule.

Scams: Regrettably, there are a lot of scams and fraudulent enterprises on the internet. To avoid being taken advantage of by these scams, you must exercise caution and due diligence. Online income can vary from month to month, with some being more profitable than others. It might be necessary for you to be ready for this and have a backup plan in case your income unexpectedly drops. In summary, making money online can be a great opportunity, but it also requires hard work, persistence, and a willingness to adapt to the ever-changing digital landscape.

Creating Reasonable Expectations

You may achieve your goals and lessen the possibility of disappointment or frustration by learning how to set realistic expectations. Define your goals and your strategy for achieving them. Unrealistic expectations may result from having hazy aims. Think about your time, resources, talents, and expertise. Realistically assessing your abilities and limitations is crucial. Remember that there are outside elements, such as market conditions, rivalry, or unforeseen events, that could affect your capacity to attain your goals. Regard the time it will take to accomplish your objectives with realism. Don't count on overnight success or quick results. As things change, be ready to modify your expectations. It's crucial to be flexible and open to changing your plan as required. Setting reasonable expectations will enable you to achieve your objectives while preventing unwarranted disappointment or frustration. Always keep in mind that long-term success and progress depend on having reasonable expectations.

Chapter 2

Launching Your Internet Business

The Niche You Want

When launching a business or producing content online, picking a niche is a crucial first step. Determine your passions and areas of interest. Start by generating ideas for activities you want to do and subjects you are enthusiastic about. Any topic is possible, from cuisine to travel, from physical fitness to personal finance. After you've determined your hobbies, conduct some research on your rivals to find out what they're up to in your specialized field. Take a look at the company's content, offerings, and intended market. Take into account the demand in your niche. Are individuals looking for information or items in your niche? Are you providing anything that is needed? Consider the demographics of the audience for your writing or goods. Take into account their age, gender, interests, and customs. By producing content or providing your audience with a good or service, you can test your niche. This will enable you to assess the level of interest and demand in your niche. Improve and correct, Refine, and modify your specialty as needed based on the input you get from your audience. This can entail adjusting your content or altering the goods or services you provide. Choosing a specialty requires time and research, keep that in mind. It's crucial to strike a balance between what you are passionate about and what is in demand in the marketplace. Finding a specialty that is both lucrative and fulfilling can be done by following these steps.

Setting Up Your Website

Although it may seem like a difficult endeavor, building a website can be a doable and even pleasurable process with the correct knowledge and techniques. Choose a purpose for your website. You need to have a firm grasp of the goal of your website before you start building it. It depends if it's a website for a company, a personal blog, or both. It will be easier for you to decide on design, content, and functionality if you are aware of the goal of your website. You don't need to know how to code to design a website because there are several free and premium website builders accessible. *Wix, Squarespace, and*

WordPress are a few popular selections. People will reach your website using your domain name, therefore it's critical to pick a name that will stick in their minds. An independent domain registrar or your website builder are also options for domain name registration. The creation of your website can begin once you have a domain name and a website builder. Choose a design or theme that is appropriate for the function of your website and then personalize it with your logo, accompanying graphics, and relevant material. Your website needs informative and interesting content, so add some. Create a blog if appropriate to the objective of your website, write engaging material for your pages, add great photographs and videos, and so on.

*Establishing Your Brand

Developing your brand entails developing a distinctive identity for your company or personal brand that distinguishes you from your rivals and generates a favorable reputation in the eyes of your target audience. *Finding your brand's core values, objectives,* and **USP** should be your first step (**USP**). By doing this, you may establish a consistent brand identity and develop a clear brand statement. Create a visual identity that embodies your company values and appeals to your target market. This involves coming up with a logo, selecting a color scheme, and picking typography that complements your brand identity. Make a good online impression by developing a website, social media accounts, and other digital channels that highlight your brand's visual identity and messaging. You will gain credibility and be able to reach a larger audience by doing this. Use blog posts, articles, podcasts, and other content formats to impart your knowledge and skills to your audience. This can help you establish credibility with your target audience and position you as an authority in your field. Engage in conversation with your audience on social media and other platforms, answer their queries, and acknowledge their contributions. You'll gain a devoted following and develop a good reputation for your brand as a result. Monitor the effectiveness of your brand and make any necessary improvements to keep it on track with your objectives and appealing to your target market.

Creating a brand requires time and work, *but if you follow these guidelines and remain consistent with your brand messaging and identity, you can create a powerful and identifiable brand that distinguishes you from competitors in your sector.*

*Configuring the Options for Payment and Shipment

A crucial step in launching an internet business is setting up payment and shipping alternatives. There are numerous ways to pay, such as *credit/debit cards, PayPal, Stripe*, and others. Find out what possibilities are available in your area, then pick the ones that will benefit your customers the best. You can accept payments online thanks to a service called a payment gateway. *PayPal, Stripe, and Authorize.net* are a few of the widely used payment processors. Choose a payment processor that works with the framework of your website. Choose which shipping companies to use and how much to charge for a shipment to your consumers. Free delivery can also be made available for purchases over a particular amount. depending on your location and the locations of your consumers, which taxes you must collect. A tax calculator might be useful in this procedure. Test your shipping and payment options before opening your online store to make sure everything is in functioning order. Make sure you abide by the rules: Be sure you abide by all applicable rules and laws about payments and delivery, including privacy and data protection legislation. Provide your consumers with clear shipping and payment alternatives. Ensure that they are aware of the shipping options, costs, and anticipated delivery dates.

Chapter 3

E-commerce and dropshipping

*Comprehension of e-commerce

The term "e-commerce," which stands for "electronic commerce," describes the exchange of products and services over the internet. It entails starting, carrying out, and finishing transactions between buyers and sellers through electronic means.

With e-commerce, companies can create an online store or offer their goods or services on already-already-established marketplaces *like Amazon, eBay, or Etsy.* Consumers can browse products, put them in their virtual shopping cart, and then purchase them using several different payment options, such as bank transfers, credit cards, debit cards, and e-wallets. The increased use of the internet and mobile devices has led to a huge increase in e-commerce over the past several years.

Customers and organizations can benefit from its convenience, accessibility, and expanded reach, among other benefits. E-commerce relieves firms of the need for physical stores, lowers overhead expenses, and enables targeted marketing. E-commerce allows users to purchase conveniently from any location, at any time, with access to a larger selection of goods at affordable prices. E-commerce does, however, also present several difficulties, including threats to cyber security, logistics and delivery, and client confidence. As a result, companies must take steps to maintain the security and safety of online transactions and gain customers' trust by offering them high-quality goods and dependable customer service.

*Selecting Items for Sale

For every business, choosing which things to sell can be a crucial choice. Choose a market that you wish to service before you start thinking about items. You will gain a better understanding of the needs and potential purchases of your customer's thanks to this. Look at the products and purchases made by your rivals' customers. This might assist you in locating market gaps that you can fill. Choose products that you are familiar with or have used before. You may be able to sell your goods more successfully and offer better customer service as a result. Search for products with significant market potential and great demand. This might assist you in making sure there is sufficient demand to support your firm. Examine the opposition to see if you have a chance to compete. It could be challenging for you to enter the market if there is too much competition. Examine the profit margins of several items to determine which are most profitable for your company. Take into account the seasonality of your products to determine whether they will likely sell well all year long or just during particular seasons, You may improve your chances of picking the correct things to offer and creating a successful business by testing your product ideas on a small sample of clients to determine whether there is enough demand for them before you spend considerably in inventory.

Chapter 4

Affiliate marketing

*What exactly is affiliate marketing

One example of performance-based marketing is affiliate marketing, in which a company pays affiliates (people or other companies) for each consumer they attract to their website through marketing activities. *Affiliates often use specific affiliate links or tracking codes to advertise a company's goods or services through their website, blog, social media accounts, email marketing, or other channels. An affiliate receives a commission on sales when customers use their affiliate link to make purchases.* A well-liked strategy for companies to increase sales and customer reach without paying significant upfront advertising expenses is affiliate marketing, which also enables affiliates to make passive money by endorsing goods they believe in.

*The search for affiliate programs

Choose the goods or services you want to advertise. If you operate a fitness blog, for instance, you might want to check for affiliate programs for nutritional supplements, exercise equipment, or gym memberships. network affiliate research Affiliate networks serve as a middleman between affiliates and merchants. Rakuten Marketing, ShareASale, and Commission Junction are a few well-known affiliate networks. You can start looking for businesses that provide affiliate programs once you've determined your specialty and selected an affiliate network. Usually, you can obtain this information by using the search bar on the affiliate network or the merchant's website. Make sure you carefully read the terms and conditions before registering for an affiliate program. Find out more about commission rates, payment periods, and promotion rules. The standing of the retailer and the caliber of the goods or services they offer should also be taken into account. You can pay to join an affiliate program after determining that it matches your needs. Typically, this entails completing an application and submitting details about your website or marketing avenues. You can begin marketing the merchant's products and earning commissions once you've been given the go-ahead.

Product Promotion Via Affiliates

Your primary objective as an affiliate marketer is to advertise goods and services to prospective clients to profit from those sales by receiving a commission. Choose goods that your audience will be interested in and that you firmly believe in. Search for items that offer high-quality content and services along with reasonable commission rates. Establish trust by producing informative content, being open about your ties, and only endorsing something you truly believe in. To reach a larger audience and increase your chances of earning sales, use a variety of marketing platforms, such as social media, email marketing, and blogging. Provide informed, interesting material that emphasizes the advantages of the product.

To give your viewers a deeper understanding of the product, including reviews, videos, and photographs. Encourage your audience to use your affiliate link to purchase by providing incentives like discounts or bonuses. Use tracking software to keep an eye on your progress and modify your marketing plan as necessary. Always keep in mind that effective affiliate marketing takes time, work, and devotion. You may raise your chances of success as an affiliate marketer by making the correct product selections, developing trust with your audience, utilizing a variety of marketing channels, producing engaging content, providing incentives, and monitoring your results.

Chapter 5

Internet Advertising

Learning About Internet Advertising

Internet advertising is the process of promoting goods, services, or concepts using electronic media like websites, social media, search engines, and mobile apps. Online advertising's primary goals are to draw in new clients and help firms produce leads, sales, and profits. *Display ads, video commercials, social media ads, search engine marketing, and email marketing* are just a few of the several formats that are frequently used for online advertising. To make sure that the correct individuals see their message at the right moment, advertisers can target their audience based on demographics, interests, habits, and other aspects. The ability to target consumers more precisely and monitor the success of advertisements is one of the benefits of online advertising. Key performance indicators, including click-through rates, conversion rates, and return on investment (ROI), may be monitored by advertisers in real time, allowing them to make necessary campaign modifications. Ad fraud, ad blocking, and privacy issues are some of the issues that online advertising must deal with. To guarantee that their efforts are effective, advertisers must be aware of these problems and take action to reduce them. Overall, online advertising has emerged as a crucial part of contemporary marketing, giving companies the chance to scale out their target audience reach and empowering customers to find new goods and services that suit their requirements and preferences.

How to Choose Your Target Market

Selecting a target market is a crucial first step in creating a marketing strategy that works. Explicitly state what your offering is, what it accomplishes, and how it helps your clients. Find out what needs and desires potential clients have that your product or service can satisfy. To learn more about the traits, actions, and preferences of your potential clients, conduct market research.

To find trends that are relevant to your product or service, look at demographic information like age, gender, income, education, and geography. Consider the psychographic variables that affect the lifestyle, values, and interests of your target audience. To find market gaps and chances to distinguish your product or service, analyze your competitors. Create thorough customer personas that accurately reflect the traits, tastes, and habits of your target audience. You may develop a marketing strategy that appeals to your target demographic by better understanding them.

How to Assess Your Advertising Success

Making educated judgments regarding future advertising tactics and determining the efficacy of your advertising campaigns depend on measuring the success of your advertising initiatives.

ROI evaluates how much money was made from an advertising campaign in comparison to the money that was spent on it. Divide the income earned by the campaign by the cost of the campaign after deducting the campaign's costs to determine the return on investment *(ROI)*. If the *ROI* is positive, the campaign was successful; if it is negative, the campaign was unsuccessful. *CPA* quantifies the expense involved in obtaining a new client through marketing efforts. Divide the cost of the campaign by the number of new consumers attracted to determine **CPA**.

*A lower **CPA** indicates more economical marketing. **CTR** gauges how many people clicked on an advertisement after seeing it.* The **CTR** is calculated by dividing the number of ad clicks by the number of impressions (**or times the ad was shown**). With a greater **CTR**, the advertisement was more interesting and pertinent to the intended audience. The conversion rate counts the number of people who performed a desired action, like making a purchase or completing a form, after clicking on an advertisement. Divide the number of conversions by the number of ad clicks to determine the conversion rate. The ability of the advertisement to elicit action is shown by a higher conversion rate. To properly understand the impact of your advertising campaigns, it's crucial to track additional indicators such as customer lifetime value, brand awareness and sentiment, and retention rates. You may optimize your advertising efforts for optimal success by routinely measuring and analyzing these KPIs and making data-driven decisions.

Chapter 6

Internet Services and Freelancing

Freelancing: A Basic Overview

The term "freelancing" describes a type of employment situation in which people carry out ad hoc, independent labor for clients. Freelancers are independent contractors who provide their services to corporations, groups, or people who need their knowledge rather than being employed by the organizations they work for. Freelancers often work from home or another distant location, and they are free to choose the jobs they wish to accomplish and the hours they work. Taxes, insurance, and other costs associated with their employees are their responsibility. Recent years have seen a rise in the popularity of freelancing as more and more people look to work independently and have more control over their professional lives. *Freelancers are in high demand across a wide range of sectors, including marketing, writing, graphic design, and programming.* Having flexibility is one of the advantages of freelancing. As they can work from anywhere in the world and frequently set their rates, freelancers can make more money than they would in typical employment. However, several difficulties come with freelancing, including the need to continually acquire new clients and manage one's workload. In conclusion, people who have the abilities and desire to thrive as independent professionals might choose to work as freelancers as a meaningful and fulfilling job.

*Discovering Freelance Employment

Getting freelance employment might be difficult, but there are several approaches you can use. It's crucial as a freelancer to present your abilities and previous work to prospective clients. You can showcase your skills and draw clients by building a portfolio website or a collection of your work on websites like **Behance or Dribbble**. There are numerous job platforms specifically for freelance employment, including Upwork, Freelancer, and Fiverr. You can use these sites to exhibit your abilities, bid on projects, and develop a clientele. *Use social media sites like Facebook, Twitter, and LinkedIn* to expand your network and establish contacts with new customers. To spread the word about yourself, participate in online forums, local events, and groups that are relevant to you. Make a list of potential customers in your niche and contact them directly with a tailored presentation. This strategy can need a little more work, but it can result in dependable clientele and work over the long run. In the realm of freelancing, word of mouth is a potent instrument. Use your current clientele to seek recommendations or testimonials so that you may show off your work to prospective customers. Bear in mind that it takes time, effort, and patience to find a freelance job. To improve your chances of success, you must be persistent and promote yourself constantly.

*Creating Your Freelance Business

A fantastic option to exercise authority over your business and operate on your terms is to launch a freelance business. Selecting a market niche in which you are knowledgeable and passionate is essential before you launch your freelance firm. This will make you stand out in a congested market and draw customers that are interested in your specialized expertise. Once you've selected your niche, specify the services you'll provide. This can include any service that fits your specialization, such as writing, editing, graphic design, site building, or social media management. Based on your level of knowledge, market demand, and the value you provide to your clients, decide on your charges. To make sure that your fees are reasonable, research the pricing of other freelancers in your niche. Your portfolio is a compilation of your finest work that demonstrates your abilities and subject matter knowledge.

Build a portfolio website with samples of your work, client endorsements, and information about your services. Building a freelancing business requires a lot of networking. To expand your network and get exposure, speak with other independent contractors in your field, go to industry events, and join online communities. It's time to start marketing your services once you've established your network and portfolio. To reach potential customers and advertise your services, use social media, email marketing, and internet advertising. You must register your company with the appropriate authorities, receive all essential licenses and permissions, open a business bank account, and maintain records of your finances to start a freelance business. Keep in mind that starting a successful freelance business requires time and work. Always endeavor to provide your clients with high-quality work by remaining persistent, keeping your goals in mind, and staying focused.

Chapter 7

Developing and Marketing Digital Goods

The various types of digital goods

Digital goods come in a variety of forms, some of which are as follows: The term "software" refers to a computer or other hardware-based programs that carry out particular tasks. Games, Adobe Photoshop, Microsoft Office, and more examples are provided.

E-books: These are books in digital form that may be read on e-readers, tablets, and cell phones. Kindle books or PDFs are a couple of examples.

Movies and films are digital files with video content that may be downloaded or watched online. Netflix movies and TV series are a few examples.

Applications for mobile devices, such as smartphones and tablets, are known as mobile applications. Apps for productivity, games, and social media are a few examples.

Digital graphics and art: These are electronic documents that may be downloaded or viewed online and feature artwork or other visual material. Digital graphics, stock pictures, and graphic design templates are some examples.

*developing digital goods

The process of developing a digital product may be exciting and gratifying. Identification of your target market and their needs is the first stage in developing a digital product. What issue or discomfort are you looking to resolve? How can you benefit your audience? Choose the format for your digital product once you have determined who your audience is and what they need. Depending on your target market and the value you are providing, this could be an e-book, an online course, a tutorial video, a mobile app, or any other digital product. The content of your digital product should be planned. This entails organizing the text into logical and understandable sections and detailing the topics. Ascertain that your content is worthwhile and pertinent to your intended audience. Start developing your digital product once your content has been planned. This requires creating the e-book, movies, software, or another format that you have selected to use. Always keep design and user experience in mind. Test your digital product extensively before releasing it to make sure it is functional and adds value for your audience. This entails looking at any technological issues, user satisfaction, and target audience input. Launch your product as soon as you are satisfied with it and begin marketing it to your intended market. To get the word out about your digital product, use email marketing, social media, and other marketing avenues. Analyze the usage of your digital product and make adjustments based on input from users and analytics. By doing this, you'll be able to fully develop your product and give your audience something useful.

*Tips for Increasing Sales

Understanding Your Target Market: It is crucial to comprehend the wants and preferences of your target market. This knowledge will enable you to better target your products and marketing initiatives for your target market. Outstanding customer service can significantly impact your sales. Be timely in your responses to customer questions, mindful of their needs, and willing to go above and beyond to ensure that they are happy with their purchase. In today's market, having competitive pricing is essential. Make sure your pricing is comparable to that of your rivals and offer incentives to draw customers, such as discounts or coupons. *A powerful tool for product promotion and audience outreach is social media.* Make use of social media sites **like Facebook, Instagram, and Twitter** to promote your products, interact with customers, and raise brand awareness. To improve your goods and services, pay attention to what your customers have to say. As a result, you will increase your customer base's loyalty and draw in more clients by spreading good word of mouth. Offering top-notch goods can help you stand out from the competition and win you repeat business. Ensure that your products are well-made, and satisfy the demands of your target market. To comprehend customer behavior, improve your sales strategies, use data analytics. You can find areas for improvements and make wise decisions about your sales by analyzing customer data.

Chapter 8

Developing and Monetizing Your Blog

*Blogging

To create online content, a person or business must consistently publish written or visual material on a blog platform or website. These articles of material, sometimes referred to as blog entries, are frequently written in a casual or conversational tone and can cover a variety of subjects, from personal experiences and opinions to news and comments on current events. Because it is so accessible and can reach a large audience, blogging has grown in popularity over time. Many bloggers use their platforms to connect with like-minded people, share their knowledge, and create communities centered around specific interests. Some bloggers even make a living off of their love of writing, generating revenue via affiliate marketing, sponsored content, and advertising. *To begin blogging, you normally need to pick a blogging platform, create a website or blog, and start regularly producing and publishing content.* Choose a market or subject that interests you deeply and has readers who are interested in reading about it. Building a devoted readership and expanding your blog over time requires consistency and sincerity. The reach and engagement of your blog can also be increased by networking with other bloggers in your niche and advertising it on social media.

Developing and Expanding Your Blog

Creating a blog can be a rewarding and enjoyable way to connect with like-minded individuals and share your ideas. Choose a particular subject or theme for your blog. This will assist you in producing content that is targeted and appropriate for your audience.

There are many blogging platforms available, including Wix, Blogger, and WordPress. Choose the platform that best suits your needs and level of expertise after researching each one. Pick a layout and style that are representative of your personality and brand. Widgets, social media icons, and other components that improve the user experience should be added. The most crucial aspect of blogging is this. Posts should be informative, interesting, and relevant to your audience. To improve your content, add images, videos, and other multimedia components. *Use channels like social media, email marketing, and others to advertise your blog and draw readers.* To expand your network, interact with other bloggers, and take part in online communities. Provide an email subscription option for your visitors to follow your blog. By doing this, you'll be able to interact with your audience on a personal level and gain their support. Track your traffic, engagement, and other important metrics using analytics tools. Use this information to optimize your blog's content and make it better over time. Be aware that blogging requires time and effort. Yet if you work hard and are persistent, you may start a popular blog, gain readers, and support your objectives.

*Making Money From Your Blog

It's possible to turn your love of writing into a source of income by monetizing your blog: Businesses that are related to your niche can purchase advertising space on your blog. This can be done either directly with advertisers or through ad networks like Google AdSense. By promoting goods or services on your blog, you can get paid. This is accomplished by integrating distinctive affiliate links into your blog posts or website banner ads. You can produce sponsored content for brands or write sponsored blog posts. However, it's crucial to only partner with companies whose values and readership mesh with your blog's. This can be a lucrative way to make money. On your blog, you can resell your goods and services. Anything from online courses and e-books to tangible goods like merchandise could fit this description. You can kindly request financial support from your readers for your blog. Members who pay a monthly or yearly fee can access exclusive content or benefits. This is a fantastic way to create a devoted following for your blog. It's crucial to strike the right balance between earning money from your blog and giving your readers useful content when monetizing it. Always put your audience first, and check that any monetization techniques you use are consistent with the goals and principles of your blog.

Tips for Increasing the Profits from Your Blog

Here are some pointers for increasing the income from your blog:

Pick the best ad network: Your revenue may be significantly impacted by the ad network you select. *AdThrive, Media.net, and Google AdSense are a few well-known ad networks.*

Find the network that best fits the audience and niche of your blog by researching and comparing various options.

Improve ad placement: The location of your blog's ads can have an impact on revenue. Ads that are placed above the fold, or at the top of the page, typically perform better than ads that are placed below the fold.

Use affiliate marketing: Affiliate marketing is the practice of promoting the goods of others in exchange for a cut of any sales generated by your special affiliate link. You can advertise goods that are appropriate for your target market and niche.

Offer premium content: You can charge for access to premium content, like e-books or online courses. Make sure the information is of high quality and pertinent to the interests of your audience.

Make use of sponsored content: You can collaborate with brands and businesses to produce sponsored content, such as sponsored posts or product reviews. Be open and honest with your audience about sponsored content, and make sure it fits the ethos and market of your blog.

Boost traffic: The more people who visit your blog, the more money you can make. To boost blog visibility and draw in more readers, use social media, SEO, and guest posting. Try out various monetization techniques and monitor the results to determine which ones are most effective for your blog. Remember that what works for one blog might not work for another, so be willing to try new things and modify your approaches as necessary.

*Final Thoughts and Online Income Strategies

about earning money online. However, based on my training data, I've come to the following general conclusions and suggested actions that you might find helpful. Making money online is possible, but it frequently takes patience, perseverance, and effort. Online businesses can be operated in a variety of ways, including **through e-commerce, affiliate marketing, and freelancing**. To find the best fit for your abilities, interests, and objectives, it's important to do your research and consider the advantages and disadvantages of each method. It's critical to have a strategy and plan in place if you want to improve your chances of success. Setting clear objectives, determining your target market, establishing a solid online presence, and continually learning about and adjusting to new trends and technologies are all part of this. *You can get more followers, clients, and opportunities by developing your brand and producing worthwhile content.* To do this, you should set up a blog, social media accounts, and other online accounts where you can display your abilities, impart knowledge, and network with others in your specialized field. It's critical to be aware of any potential scams and dangers related to earning money online. Before investing your time or money, do your homework and research any company or opportunity. Finally, keep in mind that earning money online is not a quick way to get rich. Building a sustainable online business or income stream requires time, effort, and patience. But you can achieve your financial objectives and build a fulfilling career or lifestyle online with the right mindset, knowledge, and tactics.